Practical
Steaks & Burgers

p^3

This is a P³ Book
First published in 2003

P³
Queen Street House
4 Queen Street
Bath BA1 1HE, UK

ISBN: 1-40540-940-1

Printed in China

NOTE

Cup measurements in this book are for American cups.
This book also uses imperial and metric measurements. Follow the same units
of measurement throughout; do not mix imperial and metric.
All spoon measurements are level: teaspoons are assumed to be 5 ml, and
tablespoons are assumed to be 15 ml. Unless otherwise stated,
milk is assumed to be whole milk, eggs and individual vegetables such as potatoes
are medium, and pepper is freshly ground black pepper.

The nutritional information provided for each recipe is per serving or per person.
Optional ingredients, variations, or serving suggestions have
not been included in the calculations. The times given for each recipe are an approximate
guide only because the preparation times may differ according to the techniques used by
different people and the cooking times may vary as a result of the type of oven used.

Recipes using raw or very lightly cooked eggs should be
avoided by infants, the elderly, pregnant women, convalescents,
and anyone suffering from an illness.

Contents

Introduction...4

Best-Ever Burgers 6

Thai-Style Burgers 7

Cheese Burgers 8

Cranberry Turkey Burgers 9

Lamb Burgers with Mint 10

Grilled Bean Burgers 11

Luxury Cheese Burgers....................................12

Bean Curd Burgers 13

Nutty Rice Burgers...14

Vegetable Burgers & Fries 15

Mushroom Burgers...16

Barbecue Steaks..17

Boozy Beef Steaks..18

Steaks in a Wine Marinade 19

Steaks in Orange Sauce..................................20

Tabasco Steaks 21

Mexican Steaks..22

Steak Parcels..23

Pizzaiola Steaks...24

Mustard Steaks 25

Ham Steaks with Apple Rings 26

Neapolitan Pork Steaks...................................27

Marinated Turkey Steaks.................................28

Char-Grilled Venison Steaks..........................29

Turkey Steaks with Tapenade.........................30

Spicy Lamb Steaks..31

Minted Lamb Chops...32

Introduction

Burgers and steaks are surefire winners whatever the season or occasion. Burgers are infinitely versatile and the perfect choice for an informal meal for children and adults alike. A tender beef steak, meanwhile, offers a quality eating experience and is fit for the fanciest of dinner parties, especially when served with a piquant sauce or a fruity relish on the side. Beef is only the beginning, however. In this book you can choose from a stylish range of recipes featuring ham, pork, lamb, venison, and poultry. Imaginative ideas are also included for vegetarians, so there is something here to please everyone.

Ingredients

When choosing ground meat for burgers, price is a good indication of quality. Varieties using poorer cuts that have a relatively higher proportion of fat are cheaper, but when cooked, the fat will be released from the meat and the burgers will shrink in size. Choose ground beef that has a moderate amount of fat, rather than the leanest kind, to ensure a juicy result. Ready-ground lamb and chicken can vary greatly in quality, so an excellent alternative is to home-grind your chosen meat and poultry in a meat grinder, where you can also control the texture of the finished product. A food processor can be used for the purpose, but it tends to over-grind the flesh to a pulp.

Canned beans are a marvelous convenience food and are ideal for making meat-free burgers. You can ring the changes by substituting different kinds, including kidney, cannellini, garbanzo, lima, and navy beans. Many varieties have salt and sugar added, so if you are limiting your dietary intakes of either or both, drain and rinse the beans thoroughly before using.

Meat for steaks needs to be of the tenderest quality, which means choosing cuts from areas that have had very little exercise, such as the loin or rump. The flesh should be finely grained, firm, slightly elastic, and a good, even color. Beef should be dark red tinged with brown, with a light marbling of fat. Pork should be pale pink,

instead of red. Lamb should be a slightly brownish pink—a darker color indicates an older animal and tougher flesh. If cutting your own steaks, always slice against the grain to maximize tenderness. Many factors are involved in the production and preparation of meat that determine flavor and texture, so always use a reputable supplier.

Preparation

Marinating steaks prior to cooking tenderizes and flavors the meat—a marinade usually contains an acidic ingredient, such as wine, lemon juice, vinegar, or tomatoes, which helps to break down any connective tissue. The marinade can subsequently be used for basting during cooking or for making an accompanying sauce, as long as it is thoroughly boiled to kill off any potentially harmful bacteria. Always use a nonmetallic container, such as glass or ceramic, for marinating to prevent the acid from reacting with metal. Pounding the meat between sheets of waxed paper or plastic wrap with a meat pounder or a rolling pin will also help to break down any tough fibers.

If beef or ham steaks have a skirting of fat, it should be snipped at $\frac{1}{2}$-inch/1-cm intervals with sharp kitchen scissors, otherwise the fat will shrink in the cooking process and cause the steaks to curl up.

When shaping meat or vegetable burgers, first moisten your hands with cool water to allow easier handling and to prevent the mixture from sticking.

Cooking methods and tips

Most burgers and steaks are ideal for cooking on a barbecue grill over the hottest of coals to make them deliciously charred on the outside while tender and succulent on the inside. The drippings and bastings falling on the coals vaporize and contribute that unique barbecue flavor to the food. What could be better fare for eating in the open air? To boost both the atmosphere and the taste, add your favorite aromatic wood chips to the fire, such as mesquite, hickory, or maple, or try using sprigs of woody herbs like rosemary or thyme.

As an effective indoor alternative to outdoor grilling, use a ridged griddle pan, made of cast-iron or aluminum, on the stove. Heat the dry pan slowly until very hot before adding the burgers or steak, brushed with oil or marinade to seal in the juices. Cook quickly on both sides before lowering the temperature slightly to cook through. The ridges will give an attractive "flame-grilled" effect.

If broiling, preheat the broiler on its highest setting before cooking steaks or meat burgers so that the surface quickly browns and sears on both sides before reducing to medium heat. Their maximum thickness should be about 2 inches/5 cm to prevent the outside from burning before the inside is cooked through. Pork, chicken, and turkey in particular must be thoroughly cooked through. There is some risk of food poisoning in eating rare beef, and those who are potentially vulnerable, such as the elderly, the young, invalids, and pregnant women—should avoid doing

so. Let meat come to room temperature before cooking so that it cooks evenly. Avoid seasoning steaks or burgers with salt until near the end of the cooking time, since it can have the effect of leaching the juices from the meat.

Judging the precise cooking times for broiling or grilling beef steaks in order to achieve the desired result is difficult, since the time involved in any case is only short and the size and thickness of the meat and the temperatures of different cooking appliances are highly variable. Testing the meat by piercing or cutting it is not ideal since it will cause some

of the precious juices to be lost. Try applying the touch test instead. Taking care not to burn yourself, lightly press the meat in the center of the steak with your finger. If still soft to the touch, the steak will be rare, if it feels slightly firm but still springy, this indicates medium, and if it is firm to the touch, the steak will be well done.

Healthier options

Burgers have suffered in recent times from a reputation for being highly unhealthy, and indeed many store-bought burgers—commercially produced burgers in particular—are made from poor-quality meat and are high in fat and additives. By preparing your own burgers from top-quality ingredients and by broiling, grilling, or griddling them with the minimal amount of additional fat, you will enjoy a tastier, healthier alternative. In fact, burgers made from ground turkey or chicken breast meat, in place of beef or lamb, are especially low in fat, and that fat is mostly unsaturated. For vegetarians, bean, rice, and vegetable burgers are the other healthy options on offer here.

Healthier choices can be made with steaks too. Again, turkey is tops, but venison is also very lean, although the farmed variety is less so. The leanest cuts of pork are surprisingly low in fat, containing not much more fat than that found in skinless chicken. Even lean beef contains less than 5 percent fat, the lesser proportion being saturated, and beef is a valuable source of minerals such as zinc and selenium. Be sure to trim all visible fat from beef, lamb, pork, and ham before cooking in order to reduce the fat content to a minimum.

KEY

Simplicity level 1–3 (1 easiest, 3 slightly harder)

Preparation time

Cooking time

Best-Ever Burgers

You will find that these succulent, homemade burgers bear no resemblance to the ready-made patties available in many stores.

NUTRITIONAL INFORMATION

Calories . . . . . . .659 Sugars 8g
Protein . . . . .44g Fat 26g
Carbohydrate . . .66g Saturates 5g

10 mins   6–8 mins

SERVES 6

INGREDIENTS

2 lb/900 g lean ground steak

2 onions, finely chopped

1 oz/25 g fresh white bread crumbs

1 egg, lightly beaten

1½ tsp finely chopped fresh thyme

salt and pepper

TO SERVE

6 sesame seed baps

2 tomatoes

1 onion

lettuce leaves

mayonnaise

mustard

tomato catsup

1 Preheat the barbecue grill. Place the steak, onions, bread crumbs, egg, and thyme in a large glass bowl and season to taste with salt and pepper. Mix thoroughly using your hands.

2 Using your hands and a round-bladed knife, form the mixture into 6 large patties.

3 Cook the burgers over hot coals for 3–4 minutes on each side. Meanwhile, cut the baps in half and briefly toast on the barbecue grill, cut-side down. Using a sharp knife, slice the tomatoes and cut the onion into thinly sliced rings. Fill the toasted baps with the cooked burgers, lettuce, sliced tomatoes, and onion rings and serve immediately, with the mayonnaise, mustard, and tomato catsup.

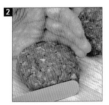

COOK'S TIP

Homemade burgers have a much looser texture than ready-made ones, so use a spatula to turn them carefully and remove them from the barbecue as soon as they are cooked.

Thai-Style Burgers

If your family likes to eat burgers, try these—they have a much more interesting flavor than conventional hamburgers.

NUTRITIONAL INFORMATION

Calories	358	Sugars	.........1g
Protein	......23g	Fat	.........29g
Carbohydrate	....2g	Saturates	.......5g

15 mins   6–8 mins

SERVES 4

INGREDIENTS

1 small lemongrass stalk

1 small fresh red chile, seeded

2 garlic cloves, peeled

2 scallions

7 oz/200 g closed-cup mushrooms

14 oz/400 g ground pork

1 tbsp Thai fish sauce

3 tbsp chopped fresh cilantro

1 tbsp all-purpose flour, for dusting

salt and pepper

sunflower oil, for cooking

2 tbsp mayonnaise

1 tbsp lime juice

TO SERVE

4 sesame seed baps

shredded napa cabbage

1 Place the lemongrass, chile, garlic, and scallions in a food processor and process to a smooth paste. Add the mushrooms and process until very finely chopped.

2 Add the ground pork, fish sauce, and cilantro. Season to taste with salt and pepper, then divide the mixture into 4 equal portions, and shape with lightly floured hands into flat burger shapes.

3 Heat the oil in a heavy skillet over medium heat. Add the burgers and cook for 6–8 minutes, until well cooked or as you like them.

4 Meanwhile, mix the mayonnaise with the lime juice. Cut the baps in half and spread the lime-flavored mayonnaise on the cut surfaces. Add a few shredded napa cabbage greens, top with a burger, and sandwich together. Serve immediately, while still hot.

COOK'S TIP

You can add a spoonful of your favorite relish to each burger or, alternatively, add a few pieces of crisp, pickled vegetables for a change of texture.

Cheese Burgers

Ground soy and seasonings combine to make these tasty vegetarian burgers, which are topped with cheese.

NUTRITIONAL INFORMATION

Calories 551   Sugars 4g
Protein . . . . .29g   Fat 24g
Carbohydrate . . .57g   Saturates 5g

🄖 🄖

🍲 1¼ hrs   🕐 10 mins

SERVES 4

I N G R E D I E N T S

5½ oz/150 g dehydrated ground soy

1¼ cups vegetable bouillon

1 small onion, finely chopped

1 cup all-purpose flour

1 egg, beaten

1 tbsp chopped fresh herbs

1 tbsp mushroom catsup or soy sauce

2 tbsp vegetable oil

4 sesame seed baps

4 cheese slices

salt and pepper

B A R B E C U E   S A U C E

2 tbsp tomato catsup

3 tbsp sweet relish

1 tbsp Worcestershire sauce

2 tsp Dijon mustard

1 tbsp white wine vinegar

2 tbsp fruity brown sauce

T O   G A R N I S H

dill pickles

tomato slices

T O   S E R V E

1 lettuce, shredded

1 cucumber, chopped

8 scallions

1 Put the ground soy into a large bowl. Pour in the vegetable bouillon and set aside to soak for about 15 minutes, until it has been absorbed.

2 Meanwhile, make the barbecue sauce. Combine the tomato catsup, relish, Worcestershire sauce, and mustard. Stir in the vinegar and fruity brown sauce, then cover and chill until required.

3 Add the onion, flour, beaten egg, and chopped herbs to the soy and mix thoroughly. Stir in the mushroom catsup or soy sauce and season to taste with salt and pepper, stirring to mix again.

4 Form the mixture into 8 burgers. Cover and chill until ready to cook.

5 Brush the burgers with oil and grill over hot coals, turning once. Cook for about 5 minutes on each side. Alternatively, cook under a preheated broiler.

6 Cut the baps in half and top one half with a burger. Lay a cheese slice on top and garnish with barbecue sauce, dill pickles, and tomato slices. Serve with a salad made with lettuce, sliced cucumber, and scallions.

Cranberry Turkey Burgers

This recipe is bound to be popular with children and is very easy to prepare for their supper.

NUTRITIONAL INFORMATION

Calories 209	Sugars 15g
Protein 22g	Fat 5g
Carbohydrate ...21g	Saturates 1g

45 mins | 25 mins

SERVES 4

INGREDIENTS

12 oz/350 g lean ground turkey

1 onion, finely chopped

1 tbsp chopped fresh sage

6 tbsp dry white bread crumbs

4 tbsp cranberry sauce

salt and pepper

1 egg white, lightly beaten

2 tsp sunflower oil

TO SERVE

4 toasted whole-wheat
  burger baps

½ lettuce, shredded

4 tomatoes, sliced

4 tsp cranberry sauce

1 Combine the turkey, onion, sage, bread crumbs, and cranberry sauce and season to taste with salt and pepper. Bind with egg white.

2 Press into 4 rounds, about ¾ inch/ 2 cm thick and 4 inches/10 cm in diameter. Chill the burgers for 30 minutes.

3 Line a broiler rack with baking parchment, making sure the ends are secured underneath the rack to ensure they do not catch fire. Place the burgers on top and brush lightly with oil. Put under a preheated moderate broiler and cook for 10 minutes. Turn the burgers over and brush again with oil. Cook for another 12–15 minutes, until cooked through.

4 Fill the burger baps with lettuce, tomato, and a burger and top with cranberry sauce.

COOK'S TIP

Look out for a variety of ready-ground meats at your butchers or supermarket. If unavailable, you can make your own by choosing lean cuts and processing them in a grinder.

Lamb Burgers with Mint

These tasty burgers have a Greek flavor. Serve them
in traditional soft baps or in pitas.

NUTRITIONAL INFORMATION

Calories 520	Sugars 4g
Protein 35g	Fat 23g
Carbohydrate ...46g	Saturates 8g

45 mins   8–10 mins

SERVES 4

I N G R E D I E N T S

1 lb/450 g lean ground lamb

1 small onion, finely chopped

1¾ oz/50 g pine nuts

2 tbsp chopped fresh mint

salt and pepper

TO SERVE

4 pitas or soft baps

2¾ oz/75 g feta cheese

salad greens

1 Place the ground lamb, chopped onion, pine nuts, fresh mint, and salt and pepper to taste in a large bowl and mix together until thoroughly combined.

2 Using your hands, divide the mixture into 4 pieces and shape the portions

into round burgers, pressing the mixture together well. Let chill in the refrigerator for 30 minutes.

3 Grill the burgers over hot coals for 4–5 minutes on each side, turning once, until the juices run clear.

4 Warm the pitas or baps at the side of the barbecue grill or toast them.

5 Crumble the feta cheese into small pieces and set aside until required.

6 Split the pitas or baps and line with the salad greens. Sandwich the burgers between the pitas or baps, and top with the crumbled feta cheese.

COOK'S TIP

If you do not have any fresh mint, use 1–2 teaspoons of mint sauce, which has a much fresher taste than dried mint. Let the burgers chill in the refrigerator before cooking them so that they become firmer and are far less likely to fall apart.

Grilled Bean Burgers

These tasty burgers are ideal for a grill in the summer, but they are equally delicious cooked indoors at any time of year.

NUTRITIONAL INFORMATION

Calories ....443 Sugars 12g
Protein ....17g Fat 14g
Carbohydrate ...68g Saturates 2g

15 mins   1 hr 5 mins

SERVES 6

I N G R E D I E N T S

¾ cup dried adzuki beans

¾ cup dried black-eye peas

6 tbsp vegetable oil

1 large onion, finely chopped

1 tsp yeast extract

¾ cup grated carrot

1½ cup fresh whole-wheat bread crumbs

2 tbsp whole-wheat flour

salt and pepper

B A R B E C U E   S A U C E

½ tsp chili powder

1 tsp celery salt

2 tbsp light brown sugar

2 tbsp red wine vinegar

2 tbsp vegetarian Worcestershire sauce

3 tbsp tomato paste

dash of Tabasco sauce

T O   S E R V E

6 whole-wheat burger buns, toasted

mixed salad

jacket potato fries

1 Place the beans and peas in separate pans, cover with water, bring to a boil, then boil for 15 minutes. Cover and simmer the adzuki beans for 25 minutes and the black-eye peas for 35 minutes. Drain the beans and peas and rinse well.

2 Transfer to a mixing bowl and lightly mash together with a potato masher or fork. Set aside.

3 Heat 1 tablespoon of the oil in a skillet and gently cook the onion for 3–4 minutes, until soft. Mix into the beans with the yeast extract, grated carrot, bread crumbs, and seasoning. Bind the mixture together well.

4 With wet hands, divide the mixture into 6 pieces and form into burgers 3¼ inches/8 cm in diameter. Put the flour on a plate and use to coat the burgers.

5 To make the barbecue sauce, mix all the ingredients together, until they are well blended.

6 Cook the burgers on a preheated medium–hot grill for 3–4 minutes on each side, brushing with the remaining oil from time to time.

7 Serve the burgers in the toasted buns with a mixed salad, fried jacket potato wedges, and the barbecue sauce.

Luxury Cheese Burgers

This is a sophisticated version of the traditional burger with a surprise filling of melted blue cheese. Serve with plenty of salad greens.

NUTRITIONAL INFORMATION

Calories 360   Sugars 4g
Protein ....32g   Fat 13g
Carbohydrate ...32g   Saturates 5g

15 mins   10 mins

SERVES 4

INGREDIENTS

2 oz/55 g Stilton cheese

1 lb/450 g lean ground steak

1 onion, finely chopped

1 celery stalk, finely chopped

1 tsp creamed horseradish

1 tbsp chopped fresh thyme

salt and pepper

TO SERVE

4 sesame seed baps

lettuce leaves

sliced tomatoes

1 Preheat the barbecue grill. Crumble the Stilton into a bowl and reserve until required. Place the steak, onion, celery, horseradish, and thyme in a separate bowl and season to taste with salt and pepper. Mix thoroughly using a wooden spoon.

2 Use your hands and a round-bladed knife to form the mixture into 8 patties. Divide the cheese between 4 of them and top with the remaining patties. Gently press together and mold the edges.

3 Cook the burgers over hot coals for 5 minutes on each side. Meanwhile, cut the baps in half and briefly toast on the barbecue, cut-side down. Fill the baps with the cooked burgers, lettuce, and tomato slices and serve immediately.

VARIATION

Substitute any blue cheese for the Stilton, and finely snipped chives for the thyme.

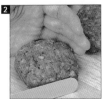

Bean Curd Burgers

Flavored with spices and served with a sesame-flavored relish, these delicious burgers are perfect for vegetarians.

NUTRITIONAL INFORMATION

Calories 471	Sugars 7g	
Protein 22g	Fat 12g	
Carbohydrate . . .74g	Saturates 2g	

15 mins   20 mins

SERVES 4

I N G R E D I E N T S

1 small red onion, finely chopped

1 garlic clove, crushed

1 tsp ground cumin

1 tsp ground coriander

2 tbsp lemon juice

1½ cups canned garbanzo beans, drained and rinsed

2¾ oz/75 g soft silken bean curd, drained

4 oz/115 g cooked potato, diced

4 tbsp chopped fresh cilantro

salt and pepper

½ cup dry whole-wheat bread crumbs

1 tbsp vegetable oil

R E L I S H

1 tsp sesame seed paste

4 tbsp lowfat unsweetened yogurt

1-inch/2.5-cm piece cucumber, finely chopped

1 tbsp chopped fresh cilantro

garlic salt, to season

T O S E R V E

2 medium tomatoes, sliced

1 large carrot, grated

4 burger baps, halved

1 Place the onion, garlic, spices, and lemon juice in a pan, bring to a boil, cover, and simmer for 5 minutes, until the onions are softened.

2 Place the garbanzo beans, bean curd, and potato in a bowl and mash well. Stir in the onion mixture, cilantro, and seasoning, and mix together. Divide the mixture into 4 equal portions and form into patties 4 inch/10 cm across.

3 Sprinkle the bread crumbs onto a plate and press the burgers into the crumbs to coat both sides.

4 Heat the oil in a large skillet and cook the burgers for 5 minutes on each side, until golden. Mix the relish ingredients together in a bowl and let chill. Place the sliced tomato, grated carrot, cooked burgers, and relish in the baps and serve.

Nutty Rice Burgers

Serve these burgers in toasted sesame seed rolls. If you wish,
add a slice of cheese to top the burger at the end of cooking.

NUTRITIONAL INFORMATION

Calories	517	Sugars	.........5g
Protein	........16g	Fat	..........26g
Carbohydrate	...59g	Saturates	.......6g

1¼ hrs   30 mins

SERVES 4

I N G R E D I E N T S

1 tbsp sunflower oil

1 small onion, finely chopped

1⅓ cups finely chopped mushrooms

2 cups cooked brown rice

1¾ cups bread crumbs

¾ cup chopped walnuts

1 egg, lightly beaten

2 tbsp brown fruity sauce

salt and pepper

dash of Tabasco sauce

vegetable oil

6 individual cheese slices (optional)

TO SERVE

6 sesame seed baps

onion slices

tomato slices

1 Heat the oil in a large pan and cook the onion for 3–4 minutes, until it just begins to soften. Add the mushrooms and cook for another 2 minutes.

2 Remove the pan from the heat. Transfer to a bowl and stir the cooked rice into the vegetables, along with the bread crumbs, walnuts, egg, brown fruity sauce, and a dash of Tabasco sauce. Season to taste and mix well.

3 Shape the mixture into 6 burgers, pressing the mixture together with your fingers. Set aside to chill in the refrigerator for at least 30 minutes.

4 Grill the burgers on an oiled rack over medium coals for 5–6 minutes on each side, turning once and frequently basting with oil. Alternatively, cook under a preheated broiler.

5 If liked, top the burgers with a slice of cheese 2 minutes before the end of the cooking time. Grill or broil the onion and tomato slices for 3–4 minutes, until they are just beginning to color.

6 Toast the sesame seed rolls at the side of the barbecue grill or under the broiler. Serve the burgers in the baps, with the onions and tomatoes.

Vegetable Burgers & Fries

These spicy vegetable burgers are delicious, especially in a warm bun or roll and served with light French fries.

NUTRITIONAL INFORMATION

Calories	.461	Sugars	.4g
Protein	.18g	Fat	.17g
Carbohydrate	.64g	Saturates	.2g

🍴 45 mins   🕐 40 mins

SERVES 4

I N G R E D I E N T S

VEGETABLE BURGERS

3½ oz/100 g spinach

2 tbsp olive oil

1 leek, chopped

2 garlic cloves, crushed

1⅓ cups chopped mushrooms

10½ oz/300 g firm bean curd, chopped

1 tsp chili powder

1 tsp curry powder

1 tbsp chopped fresh cilantro

1½ cups fresh whole-wheat bread crumbs

1 tbsp all-purpose flour, for dusting

FRENCH FRIES

2 large potatoes

2 tbsp all-purpose flour

1 tsp chili powder

2 tbsp olive oil

TO SERVE

4 burger baps

salad greens

1 To make the burgers, cook the spinach in a little boiling water for 2 minutes. Drain thoroughly and pat dry with paper towels.

2 Heat 1 tablespoon of the oil in a skillet and sauté the leek and garlic for 2–3 minutes. Add the remaining ingredients, except the bread crumbs and flour, and cook for 5–7 minutes, until the vegetables have softened. Toss in the spinach and cook for 1 minute.

3 Transfer the mixture to a food processor and process for 30 seconds, until almost smooth. Transfer to a bowl, stir in the bread crumbs, mixing well, and set aside until cool enough to handle. Using floured hands, form the mixture into 4 equal-size burgers. Chill for 30 minutes.

4 To make the French fries, cut the potatoes into thin wedges and cook in a pan of boiling water for 10 minutes. Drain thoroughly and toss in the flour and chili powder. Lay the fries on a cookie sheet and sprinkle with the oil. Cook in a preheated oven, 400°F/200°C, for 30 minutes, or until golden.

5 Meanwhile, heat the remaining oil in a skillet and cook the burgers for 8–10 minutes, turning once. Place in a bap, add some salad greens, and serve with the fries.

Mushroom Burgers

Homemade veggie burgers taste much more flavorsome—and are usually a good deal healthier—than the store-bought varieties.

NUTRITIONAL INFORMATION

Calories	164	Sugars	.........4g
Protein	.........7g	Fat	...........5g
Carbohydrate	...24g	Saturates	......1g

🍄 🍄 🍄

25 mins, plus 1 hr chilling   🕐   20 mins

SERVES 4

I N G R E D I E N T S

4 oz/115 g mushrooms

1 carrot

1 onion

1 zucchini

2 tsp sunflower oil, plus extra for brushing

1 oz/25 g peanuts

4 oz/115 g fresh white bread crumbs

1 tbsp chopped fresh parsley

1 tsp yeast extract

salt and pepper

1 tbsp all-purpose flour, for dusting

T O   S E R V E

4 oz/115 g mushrooms

1 Using a sharp knife, finely chop the mushrooms, then chop the carrot, onion, and zucchini and reserve. Heat the oil in a heavy-bottomed skillet, add the mushrooms, and cook, stirring, for 8 minutes, or until all the moisture has evaporated. Using a slotted spoon, transfer the cooked mushrooms to a large bowl.

2 Put the carrot, onion, zucchini, and peanuts into a food processor and process until finely chopped. Transfer to the bowl and stir in the bread crumbs, chopped parsley, and yeast extract. Season to taste with salt and pepper. Lightly flour your hands and form the mixture into 4 patties. Place on a large plate, cover with plastic wrap, and let chill in the refrigerator for at least 1 hour and up to 1 day.

3 Brush the mushroom burgers with sunflower oil and cook, turning, over hot coals or under a preheated broiler for 8–10 minutes. Serve with mushrooms broiled on a skewer.

VARIATION

Other nuts could also be used to make the burgers. Try cashews, hazelnuts, or even a mixture of hazelnuts and pistachios.

Barbecue Steaks

Far from being sweet, this red onion marmalade makes a delicious savory relish and an excellent accompaniment for grilled steaks.

NUTRITIONAL INFORMATION

Calories 550   Sugars 11g
Protein ....46g   Fat 31g
Carbohydrate ...14g   Saturates 10g

10 mins   30–40 mins

SERVES 4

INGREDIENTS

4 rump steaks

2 tsp wholegrain mustard

salt and pepper

2 tbsp sunflower oil

grated rind and juice of ½ orange

cooked new potatoes, to serve

RED ONION MARMALADE

2 tbsp olive oil

1 lb/450 g red onions, cut into rings

¾ cup red wine

rind of 1 orange, grated

1 tbsp superfine sugar

salt and pepper

1 To make the marmalade, place the olive oil and onions in a pan and sauté gently for 5–10 minutes, until the onions are just softened and are beginning to turn golden—do not let them overcook.

2 Add the wine, orange rind, and sugar to the pan and simmer for 10–15 minutes, until the onions are tender and most of the liquid has evaporated. Let cool, then season with salt and pepper to taste.

3 Make a few cuts in the fat around each steak to prevent it curling.

4 Using a knife, spread each steak with a little of the mustard and season with salt and pepper to taste.

5 Mix the oil with the orange juice and rind in a small bowl, and use this mixture to baste the steaks occasionally during cooking.

6 Grill the steaks over hot coals, searing the meat over the hottest part of the barbecue grill for 2 minutes on each side, basting occasionally with the orange mixture. Move the meat to an area with slightly less intense heat and cook, basting occasionally, for 4–10 minutes on each side, depending on how well done you like your steaks.

7 Transfer the steaks to plates and serve with the red onion marmalade and cooked new potatoes.

Boozy Beef Steaks

A simple marinade flavored with whiskey or brandy gives plain steaks a fabulous flavor for very little effort.

NUTRITIONAL INFORMATION

Calories 371	Sugars 5g	
Protein 48g	Fat 14g	
Carbohydrate 6g	Saturates 6g	

2¼ hrs   6–12 mins

SERVES 4

I N G R E D I E N T S

4 beef steaks

4 tbsp whiskey or brandy

2 tbsp soy sauce

1 tbsp molasses sugar

pepper

sprigs of fresh parsley, to garnish

TO SERVE

slices of tomato

garlic bread

1 Make a few cuts in the edge of fat on each steak, using a sharp knife or kitchen scissors. This will prevent the meat from curling as it cooks.

2 Place the meat in a shallow, nonmetallic dish.

3 Combine the whiskey or brandy, soy sauce, sugar, and pepper to taste in a small bowl, stirring until the sugar has dissolved. Pour the marinade over the steak, turning to coat. Cover with plastic wrap and set aside to marinate in the refrigerator for at least 2 hours.

4 Drain the steak. Grill over hot coals, searing the meat over the hottest part of the barbecue for approximately 2 minutes on each side.

5 Move the steak to an area of the barbecue with slightly less intense heat (usually the sides) and cook for another 4–10 minutes on each side, depending on how well done you like it.

6 Meanwhile, lightly grill the slices of tomato for 1–2 minutes.

7 Transfer the meat and the tomatoes to warmed serving plates. Garnish each with a sprig of fresh parsley and serve immediately with garlic bread.

Steaks in a Wine Marinade

Tenderloin, short loin, and round steak are all suitable cuts for this dish, although round steak retains the most flavor.

NUTRITIONAL INFORMATION	
Calories 356	Sugars 2g
Protein 41g	Fat 9g
Carbohydrate 2g	Saturates 4g

3 hrs   15 mins

SERVES 4

INGREDIENTS

4 round steaks, about 9 oz/250 g each

4 large portobello mushrooms

olive oil, for brushing

branch of fresh rosemary (optional)

MARINADE

2½ cups red wine

1 onion, cut into fourths

2 tbsp Dijon mustard

2 garlic cloves, crushed

salt and pepper

1 Snip through the fat strip on the steaks in 3 places, so that the steak retains its shape when cooked.

2 Combine the red wine, onion, mustard, garlic, and salt and pepper. Lay the steaks in a shallow, nonporous dish and pour over the marinade. Cover and chill in the refrigerator for 2–3 hours.

3 Remove the steaks from the refrigerator 30 minutes before you intend to cook them, to let them come to room temperature. This is especially important if the steak is thick, so that it cooks more evenly and is not well done on the outside and raw in the middle.

4 Sear both sides of the steaks—about 1 minute on each side—over a hot barbecue grill. If the steaks are about 1 inch/2.5 cm thick, keep them over a hot barbecue and cook for about 4 minutes on each side. This will give medium-rare steaks—cook them more or less, to suit your taste. If the steaks are thicker, move them to a less hot part of the barbecue or farther away from the coals.

5 Brush the mushrooms with the olive oil and cook them alongside the steak for 5 minutes, turning once. When you put the mushrooms on the barbecue grill, put the rosemary branch, if using, in the fire to flavor the meat slightly.

6 Remove the steak and set aside to rest for 1–2 minutes. Slice the mushrooms and serve with the meat.

Steaks in Orange Sauce

This is a delightful dish for a special occasion. You can use fillet or sirloin steak, because both are very tender cuts.

NUTRITIONAL INFORMATION

Calories	330	Sugars	.........9g
Protein	........38g	Fat	..........16g
Carbohydrate	....9g	Saturates	......8g

5 mins   6–8 mins

SERVES 4

INGREDIENTS

1 oz/25 g butter

4 fillet steaks, about 6 oz/175 g each

salt and freshly ground black pepper

sprigs of fresh parsley, to garnish

TO SERVE

2 large oranges

6 tbsp beef bouillon

1 tbsp balsamic vinegar

VARIATION
Substitute 1 tablespoon of orange liqueur, such as Cointreau, for 1 tablespoon of the orange juice.

1 Cut the oranges in half, then cut off 4 thin slices and reserve for the garnish. Squeeze the juice from the remaining orange halves.

2 Melt the butter in a heavy-bottomed skillet. Add the steaks and cook for 1–2 minutes on each side, or until browned and seared. Remove from the pan, season to taste with salt and pepper, set aside, and keep warm.

3 Pour the orange juice into the pan and add the beef bouillon and vinegar. Simmer over low heat for 2 minutes. Season the orange sauce to taste with salt and pepper and return the steaks to the pan. Heat through gently for about 2 minutes, or according to taste. Serve immediately, garnished with the reserved orange slices and the parsley.

Tabasco Steaks

A variation on a classic theme, this simple, but somewhat extravagant dish would be ideal for a special barbecue party.

NUTRITIONAL INFORMATION

Calories 462	Sugars 0g	
Protein 53g	Fat 28g	
Carbohydrate 0g	Saturates 16g	

10 mins   5–12 mins

SERVES 4

I N G R E D I E N T S

1 bunch of watercress, or parsley if watercress is unavailable (also see Variation below)

3 oz/85 g unsalted butter, softened

4 sirloin steaks, about 8 oz/225 g each

4 tsp Tabasco sauce

salt and freshly ground black pepper

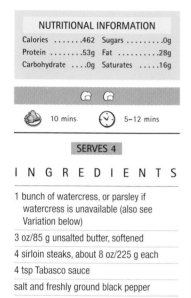 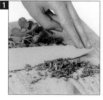 

1 Preheat the barbecue. Using a sharp knife, finely chop enough watercress or parsley to fill 4 tablespoons. Reserve a few leaves for the garnish. Place the butter in a small bowl and beat in the chopped watercress or parsley with a fork, until fully incorporated. Cover with plastic wrap and refrigerate until required.

2 Sprinkle each steak with 1 teaspoon of the Tabasco sauce, rubbing it in well. Season to taste with salt and freshly ground black pepper.

3 Cook the steaks over hot coals for 2½ minutes each side for rare, 4 minutes each side for medium, and 6 minutes each side for well done. Transfer to serving plates, garnish with the reserved leaves, and serve immediately, topped with the prepared butter.

VARIATION

If you like, substitute the same amount of fresh parsley for the watercress. Alternatively, serve the steaks with homemade or store-bought pesto sauce.

Mexican Steaks

Coated in Mexican spices and served with a refreshing
avocado salsa, these steaks will pep up your barbecue fare.

15 mins,
plus 1–2 hrs
marinating

12–24 mins

SERVES 4

INGREDIENTS

4 beef steaks

3 tbsp sunflower oil

½ red onion, grated

1 red chile, seeded and finely chopped

1 garlic clove, crushed

1 tbsp chopped fresh cilantro

½ tsp dried oregano

1 tsp ground cumin

AVOCADO SALSA

1 ripe avocado

grated rind and juice of 1 lime

1 tbsp sunflower oil

½ red onion, finely chopped

1 red chile, seeded and finely chopped

1 tbsp chopped fresh cilantro

salt and pepper

1 Make a few cuts in the edge of fat around each steak to prevent the meat from curling as it cooks. Place the meat in a shallow, nonmetallic dish.

2 Combine the oil, onion, chile, garlic, cilantro, oregano, and cumin in a small bowl. Pour the marinade over the steaks, turning the meat so that it is well coated. Let marinate for 1–2 hours.

3 To make the salsa, halve the avocado and remove the pit. Peel and dice the flesh into small cubes. Combine the avocado with the lime rind and juice, oil, onion, chile, cilantro, and salt and pepper to taste, and mix well. Cover and let chill in the refrigerator until required.

4 Grill the steaks on an oiled rack over hot coals for 6–12 minutes on each side, until cooked to your taste.

5 Serve the steaks accompanied by the avocado salsa.

VARIATION

The avocado salsa can also be served with chicken. Reduce the amount of chile if you want a milder flavor. If fresh chiles are not available, look out for jars of minced chiles, which are a good substitute.

Steak Parcels

A red wine marinade is perfect for steak, because it imparts a delicious flavor and tenderizes the meat to a melt-in-the-mouth consistency.

NUTRITIONAL INFORMATION		
Calories 466	Sugars 2g	
Protein 54g	Fat 21g	
Carbohydrate 3g	Saturates 9g	

10 mins, plus 8 hrs marinating

10 mins

SERVES 4

INGREDIENTS

4 sirloin or rump steaks

1 oz/25 g butter

2 tsp Dijon mustard

4 shallots, finely chopped

4 sprigs of fresh thyme

MARINADE

1¼ cups dry red wine

2 tbsp olive oil

salt and pepper

6 bay leaves

1 Place the steaks in a large, shallow, nonmetallic dish. Mix the wine and oil together in a pitcher and season to taste with salt and pepper. Pour the marinade over the steaks, top with 2 bay leaves, cover with plastic wrap, and let marinate in the refrigerator for up to 8 hours.

2 Preheat the barbecue. Cut out 4 squares of foil large enough to enclose the steaks and coat the centers with the butter and mustard. Drain the steaks and place them on the foil squares. Top with the shallots, thyme, and remaining bay leaves and fold over the foil to make neat parcels.

3 Cook the parcels over hot coals for 10 minutes, turning once. Serve the steaks immediately in the parcels.

VARIATION
If you like, substitute the same amount of creamed horseradish for the mustard and use fresh marjoram sprigs instead of the thyme.

Pizzaiola Steaks

The Neapolitan sauce in this dish uses the delicious red tomatoes so abundant around Naples, but canned ones make an excellent alternative.

NUTRITIONAL INFORMATION

Calories	371	Sugars	.........7g
Protein	........43g	Fat	..........19g
Carbohydrate	....7g	Saturates	.......5g

25 mins   30 mins

SERVES 4

I N G R E D I E N T S

4 thin sirloin or rump steaks

fresh herbs, to garnish (optional)

sautéed potatoes and a cooked green vegetable, to serve

N E A P O L I T A N S A U C E

1 lb 12 oz/800 g canned peeled tomatoes, or 1 lb 10 oz/750 g fresh tomatoes

4 tbsp olive oil

2–3 garlic cloves, crushed

1 onion, finely chopped

1 tbsp tomato paste

salt and pepper

1½ tsp chopped fresh marjoram or oregano, or ¾ tsp dried marjoram or oregano

2 tbsp chopped fresh parsley

1 tsp sugar

1 If using canned tomatoes, puree them in a food processor, then sieve to remove the seeds. If using fresh tomatoes, skin, remove the seeds, and chop finely.

2 Heat half of the oil in a pan and cook the garlic and onion very gently for about 5 minutes, or until softened.

3 Add the tomatoes, seasoning, tomato paste, and herbs to the pan. If using fresh tomatoes, add 4 tablespoons of water.

Simmer very gently for 8–10 minutes, giving an occasional stir.

4 Meanwhile, trim the steaks if necessary, then season. Heat the remaining oil in a skillet and cook the steaks quickly on both sides to sear, then continue until cooked to your taste— 2 minutes for rare, 3–4 minutes for medium, or 5 minutes for well done. Alternatively, cook the steaks under a hot broiler after brushing lightly with oil.

5 When the sauce has thickened a little, adjust the seasoning and stir in the chopped parsley and the sugar.

6 Pour off the excess fat from the pan containing the steaks and add the tomato sauce. Reheat gently and serve at once, with the sauce spooned over and around the steaks. Garnish with sprigs of fresh herbs, if using. Sautéed potatoes and a cooked green vegetable make very good accompaniments.

Mustard Steaks

Tarragon mustard gives these steaks a subtle spicy flavor that contrasts well with the sharp taste of the sweet-and-sour tomato relish.

NUTRITIONAL INFORMATION

Calories 380	Sugars 17g	
Protein 54g	Fat 11g	
Carbohydrate ...18g	Saturates 5g	

10 mins, plus 1 hr cooling/standing   50–60 mins

SERVES 4

INGREDIENTS

4 sirloin or rump steaks

1 tbsp tarragon mustard

2 garlic cloves, crushed

sprigs of fresh tarragon, to garnish

TOMATO RELISH

8 oz/225 g cherry tomatoes

2 oz/55 g raw brown sugar

2 fl oz/50 ml white wine vinegar

1 piece of preserved ginger, chopped

½ lime, thinly sliced

salt

1 To make the tomato relish, place all the ingredients in a heavy-bottomed pan, seasoning to taste with salt. Bring to a boil, stirring, until the sugar has completely dissolved. Lower the heat and simmer, stirring occasionally, for 40 minutes, or until thickened. Transfer to a bowl, cover with plastic wrap, and let cool.

2 Preheat the barbecue. Using a sharp knife, cut almost completely through each steak horizontally to make a pocket. Spread the mustard inside the pockets and rub the steaks all over with the garlic. Place the steaks on a plate, cover with plastic wrap, and let stand for 30 minutes.

3 Cook the steaks over hot coals for 2½ minutes each side for rare, 4 minutes each side for medium, or 6 minutes each side for well done. Transfer to serving plates, garnish with fresh tarragon sprigs, and serve immediately with the tomato relish.

COOK'S TIP
Use long-handled tongs to turn the steaks over. Try to avoid using a fork because this will pierce the meat and some of the delicious juices will be lost.

Ham Steaks with Apple Rings

This dish is quick to prepare because there is no marinating involved.
Ham has a good, strong flavor and cooks well on the barbecue.

NUTRITIONAL INFORMATION

Calories 358	Sugars 13g	
Protein 31g	Fat 21g	
Carbohydrate ...13g	Saturates 8g	

15 mins   6–8 mins

SERVES 4

INGREDIENTS

4 ham steaks, each about 6 oz/175 g

1–2 tsp wholegrain mustard

1 tbsp honey

2 tbsp lemon juice

1 tbsp sunflower oil

APPLE RINGS

2 green eating apples

2 tsp raw brown sugar

¼ tsp ground nutmeg

¼ tsp ground cinnamon

¼ tsp ground allspice

1–2 tbsp melted butter

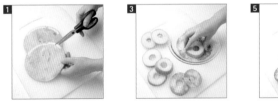

1 Using a pair of scissors, make a few cuts around the edges of the ham steaks to prevent them from curling up as they cook. Spread a little wholegrain mustard over the steaks.

COOK'S TIP

Ham can be a little salty. If you have time, soak the steaks in cold water for 30–60 minutes before cooking—this process will remove the excess salt.

2 Mix together the honey, lemon juice, and oil in a bowl.

3 To prepare the apple rings, core the apples and cut them into thick slices. Mix the sugar with the spices and press the apple slices in the mixture, until well coated on both sides.

4 Grill the ham steaks over hot coals for 3–4 minutes on each side, basting with the honey and lemon mixture

to prevent the meat from drying out during cooking.

5 Meanwhile, brush the apple slices with a little melted butter and grill them alongside the ham steaks for 3–4 minutes, turning once, and brushing with melted butter as they cook.

6 Serve the ham steaks with the apple slices as a garnish.

Neapolitan Pork Steaks

This dish is an Italian version of broiled pork steaks.
It is easy to make and delicious to eat.

NUTRITIONAL INFORMATION

Calories	353	Sugars	........3g
Protein	........39g	Fat	..........20g
Carbohydrate	....4g	Saturates	.......5g

10 mins   20 mins

SERVES 4

INGREDIENTS

2 tbsp olive oil

1 garlic clove, chopped

1 large onion, sliced

14 oz/400 g canned tomatoes

2 tsp yeast extract

4 pork loin steaks, each about 4½ oz/125 g

2¾ oz/75 g black olives, pitted

2 tbsp shredded fresh basil

Parmesan cheese, freshly grated, to garnish

freshly cooked vegetables, to serve

1 Heat the oil in a large skillet. Add the garlic and onion and cook, stirring, for 3–4 minutes, or until they just begin to soften.

2 Add the canned tomatoes and yeast extract to the skillet and simmer for about 5 minutes, or until the sauce starts to thicken.

3 Cook the pork steaks under a preheated broiler for 5 minutes on both sides, until the meat is cooked through. Set the pork aside and keep warm.

4 Add the olives and fresh shredded basil to the sauce in the skillet and stir quickly to combine.

5 Transfer the steaks to warm serving plates. Top the steaks with the sauce, sprinkle with freshly grated Parmesan cheese, and serve with cooked vegetables.

COOK'S TIP
Parmesan is a mature and exceptionally hard cheese produced in Italy. You need to add only a little because it has a very strong flavor.

Marinated Turkey Steaks

Prepare these steaks the day before they are needed and serve in toasted ciabatta bread, accompanied by crisp salad greens.

NUTRITIONAL INFORMATION	
Calories 219	Sugars 4g
Protein 28g	Fat 10g
Carbohydrate 4g	Saturates 1g

12 hours   15 mins

SERVES 4

INGREDIENTS

4 turkey breast steaks

salt and pepper

MARINADE

3½ oz/100 g red currant jelly

2 tbsp lime juice

3 tbsp olive oil

2 tbsp dry white wine

¼ tsp ground ginger

pinch grated nutmeg

TO SERVE

mixed salad greens

vinaigrette dressing

1 ciabatta loaf

baby plum tomatoes, halved

COOK'S TIP

Turkey and chicken escalopes are also ideal for cooking on the barbecue. Since they are thin, they cook through without burning on the outside. Leave them overnight in a marinade of your choice then cook, basting with a little lemon juice and oil.

1 Place the red currant jelly and lime juice in a pan and heat gently, until the jelly melts. Add the oil, wine, ginger, and nutmeg.

2 Place the turkey steaks in a shallow, nonmetallic dish and season with salt and pepper. Pour over the marinade, turning the meat so that it is well coated. Cover and refrigerate overnight.

3 Remove the turkey from the marinade, reserving the marinade for basting. Grill on an oiled rack over hot coals for about 4 minutes on each side, basting the turkey steaks frequently with the reserved marinade.

4 Meanwhile, toss the salad greens in the vinaigrette dressing. Cut the ciabatta loaf in half lengthwise and place, cut-side down, at the side of the grill. Cook until golden. Place each steak on top of some salad greens, sandwich between 2 pieces of bread, and serve with baby plum tomatoes.

Char-Grilled Venison Steaks

Venison has a good strong flavor, which makes it an ideal meat
to barbecue. Marinate overnight to tenderize the meat.

12 hours   25 mins

SERVES 4

INGREDIENTS

4 venison steaks

MARINADE

⅔ cup red wine

2 tbsp sunflower oil

1 tbsp red wine vinegar

1 onion, chopped

few sprigs of fresh parsley

2 sprigs of fresh thyme

1 bay leaf

1 tsp superfine sugar

½ tsp mild mustard

salt and pepper

TO SERVE

jacket potatoes

salad greens and cherry tomatoes

1. Place the venison steaks in a shallow, nonmetallic dish.

2. Combine the wine, oil, wine vinegar, onion, fresh parsley, thyme, bay leaf, sugar, mustard, and salt and pepper to taste in a bowl or screw-top jar and stir or shake vigorously, until well combined. Alternatively, using a fork, whisk the ingredients together in a bowl.

3. Pour the marinade mixture over the venison, cover, and let marinate in the refrigerator overnight. Turn the steaks over in the mixture occasionally so that the meat is well coated.

4. Cook the venison over hot coals, searing the meat over the hottest part of the grill for about 2 minutes on each side.

5. Move the meat to an area with slightly less intense heat and grill for another 4–10 minutes on each side, depending on how well done you like your steaks.

6. Serve with jacket potatoes, salad greens, and cherry tomatoes.

Turkey Steaks with Tapenade

Sun-dried tomatoes have a marvelously rich, fruity flavor, which perfectly complements the marinated turkey in this dish.

NUTRITIONAL INFORMATION

Calories	520	Sugars	.........2g
Protein	........44g	Fat	..........34g
Carbohydrate	....4g	Saturates	......5g

10 mins, plus
1 hr marinating

10–15 mins

SERVES 4

I N G R E D I E N T S

4 turkey steaks

M A R I N A D E

⅔ cup white wine

1 tbsp white wine vinegar

1 tbsp olive oil

1 garlic clove, crushed

1 tbsp chopped fresh parsley

pepper

T A P E N A D E

8 oz/225 g sun-dried tomatoes
in oil, drained

4 canned anchovy fillets, drained

1 garlic clove, crushed

1 tbsp lemon juice

3 tbsp chopped fresh parsley

COOK'S TIP

Always marinate the meat in
a nonmetallic bowl because the
marinade usually contains acidic
ingredients, such as vinegar or wine.
These may react with a metal bowl
and taint the flavor of the meat.

1 Place the turkey steaks in a shallow, nonmetallic dish. Mix all the marinade ingredients together in a pitcher, whisking well to mix. Pour the marinade over the turkey steaks, turning to coat. Cover with plastic wrap and marinate in the refrigerator for at least 1 hour.

2 Preheat the barbecue. To make the tapenade, put all the ingredients into a food processor and process to a smooth paste. Transfer to a bowl, cover with plastic wrap, and chill in the refrigerator until required.

3 Drain the turkey steaks, reserving the marinade. Cook over medium hot coals for 10–15 minutes, turning and brushing frequently with the reserved marinade. Transfer to 4 large serving plates and top with the sun-dried tomato tapenade. Serve immediately.

Spicy Lamb Steaks

Lamb, fresh rosemary, and bay leaves always go well together, and in this dish a hot and spicy marinade gives the lamb an extra special flavor.

NUTRITIONAL INFORMATION

Calories 490	Sugars 20g	
Protein 39g	Fat 28g	
Carbohydrate . . .23g	Saturates 9g	

15 mins, plus
3 hrs 20 mins
cooling/marinating

40 mins

SERVES 4

INGREDIENTS

4 lamb steaks, about 6 oz/175 g each

8 sprigs of fresh rosemary

8 fresh bay leaves

2 tbsp olive oil

SPICY MARINADE

2 tbsp sunflower oil

1 large onion, finely chopped

2 garlic cloves, finely chopped

2 tbsp jerk seasoning

1 tbsp curry paste

1 tsp grated fresh gingerroot

14 oz/400 g canned chopped tomatoes

4 tbsp Worcestershire sauce

3 tbsp light raw brown sugar

salt and pepper

1 To make the marinade, heat the oil in a heavy-bottomed pan. Add the onion and garlic and cook, stirring occasionally, for 5 minutes, or until softened. Stir in the jerk seasoning, curry paste, and ginger and cook, stirring constantly, for 2 minutes. Add the tomatoes, Worcestershire sauce, and sugar, then season to taste with salt and pepper. Bring to a boil, stirring constantly, then lower the heat and simmer for 15 minutes, or until thickened. Remove from the heat and let cool.

2 Place the lamb steaks between 2 sheets of plastic wrap and beat with the side of a rolling pin to flatten. Transfer the steaks to a large, shallow, nonmetallic dish. Pour the marinade over them, turning to coat. Cover with plastic wrap and marinate in the refrigerator for 3 hours.

3 Preheat the barbecue. Drain the lamb, reserving the marinade. Cook the lamb over medium hot coals, brushing frequently with the marinade, for 5–7 minutes on each side. Meanwhile, dip the rosemary and bay leaves in the olive oil and cook on the barbecue grill for 3–5 minutes. Serve the lamb immediately with the herbs.

VARIATION

Many different marinades will work equally well for this lamb dish, such as the white wine marinade on page 30, so try experimenting with different flavors.

Minted Lamb Chops

You can use any kind of lamb chops—leg chops are very tender—or cutlets, in which case you will need two per serving. Shoulder steaks also work well.

NUTRITIONAL INFORMATION

Calories	420	Sugars	.........1g
Protein	........30g	Fat	..........33g
Carbohydrate	....1g	Saturates	.....15g

15 mins, plus
2 hrs marinating

10–14 mins

SERVES 6

INGREDIENTS

6 chump chops, about 6 oz/175 g each

1 tbsp olive oil, plus extra for brushing

1 tbsp orange juice

1 tsp walnut oil

2 tbsp chopped fresh mint

MARINADE

⅔ cup thick plain yogurt

2 garlic cloves, finely chopped

1 tsp grated fresh gingerroot

¼ tsp coriander seeds, crushed

salt and pepper

1 Place the chops in a large, shallow, nonmetallic bowl. To make the marinade half of the yogurt in a pitcher

VARIATION

If you like, omit the orange juice and walnut oil and stir in ¼ teaspoon ground star anise and a pinch each of ground cinnamon and ground cumin.

and mix with the garlic, ginger, and coriander seeds. Season to taste with salt and pepper. Spoon the mixture over the chops, turn until well coated, cover with plastic wrap, and marinate in the refrigerator for 2 hours. Turn occasionally.

2 Preheat the barbecue. Place the remaining yogurt in a small bowl with the olive oil, orange juice, walnut oil, and

mint. Using a hand-held whisk, whisk until thoroughly blended. Season to taste. Cover the minted yogurt with plastic wrap and refrigerate until ready to serve.

3 Drain the chops, scraping off the marinade. Brush with olive oil and then cook over medium hot coals for 5–7 minutes on each side. Serve immediately with the minted yogurt.